PAC
4/01

the extreme sports collection

skateboarding!

surf the pavement

by L. M. Burke

rosen publishing group's

rosen central

new york

Special thanks to Ben Liversedge.

Published in 1999 by The Rosen Publishing Group, Inc.
29 East 21st Street, New York, NY 10010

First Edition

Library of Congress Cataloging-in-Publication Data

Burke, L. M.
    Skateboarding! Surf the pavement / L. M. Burke. —1st ed.
       p.   cm. — (The extreme sports collection)
    Includes bibliographical references (p. 58) and index.
    Summary: Describes the origins and evolution, equipment and techniques of the sport known as "sidewalk surfing."
    ISBN 0-8239-3014-9
    1. Skateboarding Juvenile literature. 2. Extreme sports Juvenile literature. [1. Skateboarding.]   I. Title. II. Title: Skateboarding!   III. Series.
GV859.8.B87   1999
796.22—dc21   99-24306
                                                  CIP

Manufactured in the United States of America

contents

What's Extreme?

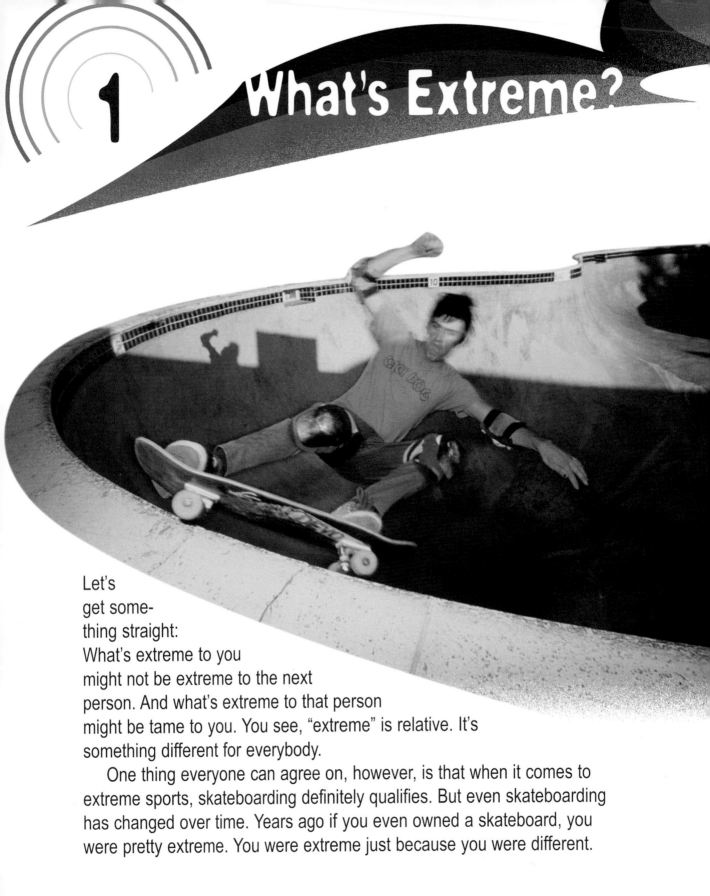

Let's
get some-
thing straight:
What's extreme to you
might not be extreme to the next
person. And what's extreme to that person
might be tame to you. You see, "extreme" is relative. It's
something different for everybody.

One thing everyone can agree on, however, is that when it comes to
extreme sports, skateboarding definitely qualifies. But even skateboarding
has changed over time. Years ago if you even owned a skateboard, you
were pretty extreme. You were extreme just because you were different.

Skaters get huge air on the halfpipe at the X Games.

Today it's not that simple. Millions of people skateboard. To be an extreme skater nowadays, you not only have to have a skateboard, but you also have to know how to use it to do the biggest ollies and the wildest tricks, and do them in style. That's extreme.

Today there are the X Games, a sort of miniature Olympics for extreme sports. Athletes from around the world gather for this event to show just how extreme they can be. They climb ice walls, race down slippery, snow-covered ski slopes on mountain bikes, and jump out of airplanes with skateboards strapped to their feet. They compete to see who can grab the biggest air, who

can hit the highest speeds, and who can perform the most difficult stunts. The winners are given gold medals and the title of "Most Extreme Athlete on the Planet." The most extreme, that is, until the next X Games, when new athletes redefine what it means to be extreme.

Another version of extreme sports takes place behind the scenes, away from the glory that comes with television coverage and cheering crowds. These athletes prefer to play alone, with only nature and the elements for company. They're the mountain climbers, the backcountry bikers and snowboarders, the explorers. They'll never get a gold medal for what they do, and they probably wouldn't want one anyway. They're doing what they do because they love it, not because it attracts a crowd.

Let's face it—most of us want things fast, loud, and dangerous. Things like school and work make us follow rules and behave. We need an outlet to be

Ollieing this car is definitely an extreme stunt, but it's also extremely dangerous.

able to enjoy ourselves. We look for ways of expressing ourselves creatively in order to get a sense of who we are and what we're capable of. This is a safe way to feel good. Art, music, and sports are safe outlets. Extreme sports can be dangerous, but with practice and the right safety precautions, they're just like any other sport. Anyone can participate in extreme sports. Some sports may be less or more extreme than others, but we can all enjoy the excitement of feeling extreme.

Part of the thrill of extreme sports is that they can be dangerous, but being extreme doesn't mean being foolish or taking unnecessary risks. No skateboarder wants to risk an injury that might mean never skating again. You can be extreme and still follow safety rules.

Extreme sports allow us to test our limits. How far can you go?

How fast can you skate? How soon before you're
exhausted? One more trick, one more jump. Is it the dan-
ger? Is it not knowing if you'll come out of that next trick with
or without a broken bone? Maybe that's a little too extreme
for most people. Most of us want our thrills without too much
risk. With skateboarding you can be as extreme as you want to
be. If you just want a small taste of excitement, skateboarding
can be a great experience. You can skate at your own pace and
maybe try a few tricks when you're ready. However, if you want to
go all the way and see how extreme you can be, skateboarding is
also perfect for you.

Skateboarding has no boundaries. With practice you can take it
to the extreme!

Old-school skater Mike McGill ollie grabs the gap

2

Skateboarding's Roots

You may think that skateboarding is a relatively new sport, but it actually has been around for quite some time. It has gone through a few changes to become the extreme sport we know today.

Today skateboarders are flying high above ramps called halfpipes or turning regular city streets into skateboarding playgrounds. But if you look closely, skateboarders have been around practically forever. Who knows, your grandparents or great-grandparents might have been skaters!

At the beginning of the twentieth century, roller-skating became popular. Roller skates then were quite different from today's in-line skates. Each skate had two sets of two wheels, side by side under each foot. At that time, roller-skating was mainly an activity for girls.

But if a girl had a brother, there was a good chance that he would sneak into her room and swipe her skates. He would remove the wheels and fasten them to the bottom of a narrow wooden board. Then he would fasten a wooden crate—the kind that vegetables or fruit might come in—to the board. The result was a homemade scooter. Store-bought scooters also could be made into skateboards just by removing the pushbar. Scooters were the first step in the evolution of skateboards. It was only a matter of time before the crates were removed and the riders were balancing on the

boards. Soon these modified scooters came to be called skateboards.

During the 1950s a surfer named Bill Richards and his son, Mark, who also surfed, hit upon the idea of using homemade skateboards to "surf" the sidewalks on days when the waves weren't right for water surfing. The idea caught on among surfing enthusiasts and eventually among young people all over the United States. Sporting goods manufacturers such as Hobie began

producing skateboards that
could be found in department stores
everywhere. Skateboarding's popularity grew
steadily until the mid-sixties, when the sport began
to develop the reputation of being unsafe. Many
stores stopped selling skateboards, and the sport went
into its first slump. Some devoted skaters were still
around, but skateboarding was no longer the popular activity
that it had been.

In the early 1970s, skateboarding began to come back into
style. This time skateboards were being made of plastic. Plastic
skateboards were sold in toy stores and sporting goods stores. They
were very narrow, hardly big enough for your feet, and not even two
feet long. The wheels were slow, and you couldn't do very much with
them in the way of tricks. They were most popular in California, where a
well-established surfing community already existed.

In 1973, a surfer named Frank Nasworthy invented wheels made from
urethane, a hard, sturdy plastic. These wheels changed skateboarding forever by making it possible for riders to go faster, control their boards better,
and spend more time on the board. Urethane wheels also helped make it

possible for skaters to jump over obstacles or do jumps and twists in midair.

As more and more skaters learned to ollie and do other tricks, doctors, parents, and other nonskaters became concerned about the risk of skateboarding injuries. Many people began to think of skateboarding as a dangerous sport, and some parents refused to let their kids skate. By 1978 skateboarding had entered its second major slump in popularity. The slump lasted until about 1982, when skating again came back into style.

Skater Bio

Tony Hawk is among the best known and most successful skateboarders in the history of the sport. He has set and continues to set many of the standards in skate-boarding. In the early 1980s, Tony helped make skate-boarding popular again with his skill and style. Tony regularly dominates pro-fessional competitions in both street skating and vert (ramp) skat-ing events. He and Andy Macdonald, another veteran, or "old-school," skater who is still going strong, rule the vert doubles event at the X Games. Tony started skating when he was in his teens, won his first competition in 1982, and is expected to keep skating and winning well into his thirties. He also has his own skateboard company, Birdhouse, which sponsors a professional team.

Sidewalk Surfing

Surfing had a huge impact on skating, and skateboarders got some of their style from surfing. In fact, skateboarding was sometimes called sidewalk surfing. It looks similar to riding a surfboard, but the similarities aren't as strong as they may seem. Surfing is restricted to water, but even though skateboarding is restricted to land, anything can become a skater's wave.

Soon skaters who were cruising the streets of California beach communities like Santa Monica and Santa Cruz were making all kinds of street objects their own personal oceans. A park bench was no longer just a park bench but something to jump over, across, or onto. Obstacles were no longer just obstacles but also the potential source of a new trick. As skateboarding became more and more popular in the early 1980s, the boards became wider, and the phenomenon started to spread inland from the coast.

Skateboarding catapulted into every household with the release of the movie *Back to the Future* in 1985. It starred Michael J. Fox as Marty McFly, a skateboarding time-traveler. Seemingly overnight every toy store in America began selling skateboards. Soon it seemed as if kids were skateboarding up and down every Main Street in America—sometimes to the dismay of their parents, local authorities, and pedestrians.

At the same time that skateboarding was becoming popular with kids all across America and amateurs were rolling around everywhere, the California kids who had been skating since the beginning were getting better and better at it. They were on their way to becoming pros. They were now jumping through the air and lifting their boards under their feet, doing a trick called an ollie. An ollie is the most basic of skateboarding tricks, and it is what most other street tricks are based on. (There will be more about ollies in chapter four.)

Marty McFly skates into the future in *Back to the Future 2.*

Alan "Ollie" Gelfand in the pool
at Winchester skate park, 1979

Skating Gets Serious

Now that almost every kid in America seemed to be tearing up his or her neighborhood streets, the level of competition increased, and soon neighborhood kids from all over were becoming professional skaters. Skateboarding had gained a foothold in the world of American sports, with organized competitions and corporate sponsorship.

Unfortunately, many adults still thought of skateboarding as a hobby practiced by juvenile delinquents. Skateboarding was often associated with vandalism and troublemaking kids. In many towns across the country, the sport was outlawed, and the local police confiscated skateboards.

Still, kids kept skating, and gradually skaters began to be viewed as

Is Skateboarding a Crime?

More than any other sport, skateboarding is seen by many people as an outlaw sport, a pastime for "bad" kids. Where does this reputation come from? It's not completely clear, but it may have something to do with the risks and potential dangers of the sport. Street skaters in particular risk injuring not only themselves but also passersby, and skate parks often have trouble finding insurance because of the fear that skaters might seriously injure themselves or others. It's true that skaters can get hurt, sometimes seriously or even fatally, but several other sports, including football and bicycling, have greater percentages of injuries per year than skateboarding does.

Then there's the music. For years many skaters have listened to punk and ska, which lots of people consider too loud and aggressive. The outrageously baggy clothes that some skaters wear make them stand out in a crowd and add to skateboarding's reputation as a sport for rebels. And in lots of cities and towns, skating on public streets is illegal, so skaters in those places may literally be lawbreakers.

Fortunately more and more cities across the United States and Canada are beginning to view skating as a sport rather than a criminal act. Many are allowing skate parks, where people can skate without worrying about cars, pedestrians, or uneven, skin-eating pavement. That's all most skaters want: a place to thrash hard, skate safely, and have fun.

The extreme mother-daughter skate team Juliann and Bethany Andreen competed at the 1998 X Games.

athletes rather than outlaws. In the last few years, skateboarding has finally earned the respect of the sports community. Professional skateboarders tour the globe putting on shows and performing in competitions sponsored by some of the world's biggest companies. Professionals earn good salaries, and some skaters even start their own companies that manufacture skateboards and clothing.

Skateboarding has come a long way since its humble beginnings on the streets of California. What started out as a local trend has now become one of the most popular sports in the world.

3

Safety First

We all know the saying "Don't try this at home." With skateboarding there's a reason to listen to that saying. When you see the pros on television or at a competition making the tricks look easy, it's because they have been training hard for a long time. The only way to learn how to pull off the big tricks is with practice, patience, and most important, attention to all the rules of safety before going out on the street or riding a ramp. Remember that if you don't wear your safety gear, you won't be around to get good at skateboarding—or anything else.

The most important safety gear is your head—not the outside, but the inside. Use

Without his helmet, pro skater Chris Senn would be in big trouble right about now.

One, two, three: the anatomy of a bail. Sergie Ventura falls during his run on the halfpipe.

your brain when deciding what safety gear to use and what tricks you can pull off safely.

Safety gear can cover almost every part of your body. Some of it is necessary at different times and at different levels of skateboarding. When skating, you want to be careful to keep your body protected from scrapes, bruises, fractures, and breaks. However, wearing so much gear that you cannot move properly also can cause injury by slowing down your reflexes and reactions.

The Art of Falling Down

Okay. Let's be real. You can't skate without getting hurt. At first you're going to fall down...a lot. The only way to get used to balancing on the board is to get back on it every time it flies out from underneath you. In chapter four we'll talk about how not to fall down, and also how—when you do fall—to fall properly and do the least damage to yourself and others.

Falling down is an unavoidable part of being a beginner, but there are ways to avoid being seriously injured in a fall. The first way is to use the right safety gear. Putting pads in the right places will keep away the worst of the scrapes, bruises, fractures, and breaks.

If you scrape your knee or anything else on the ground, it might not seem like a big deal. But if the skin breaks and you start to bleed, make sure to go home and have the scrape taken care of immediately. It may not hurt, but it can become serious if you keep on skating. If a scrape isn't cleaned properly and promptly, dirt and bacteria from the ground and your sweat can get into the open wound and cause it to become infected. If the scrape becomes infected, it will swell and hurt, and you'll have to go to the doctor for antibiotics. You can avoid all that unpleasantness by being responsible. It's not cool to bleed or have scars. If you do cut yourself and are bleeding, see an adult immediately so that he or she can determine whether the wound is serious. If you are punctured or sliced by an object—especially a metal one—go to an emergency room immediately. You may need a tetanus shot. If the wound does not stop bleeding, you may need stitches to help the skin heal.

Safety Tip

"If you do get a scrape, you'll want to clean it right away," says Dr. David Sekons at Beth Israel Medical Center in New York City. Once an adult has determined that it's not serious, here's what Dr. Sekons says to do:

1. Go home immediately. The faster you get it taken care of, the faster you can get back on your skateboard.

2. Remove any clothing that is touching the wound. You'll need to remove anything near the scrape. If the scrape occurred under your clothing, very gently peel away the material. If it hurts too much, wetting the area will help.

3. Clean the scrape's surface. Use a clean wet cloth to remove all of the surface dirt and blood from the scrape. Don't worry—with all the dirt and blood, the scrape probably looks worse than it is. Gently wipe away the dirt. It may hurt to touch the wound with the cloth, so try to wipe around it, but get all the dirt away from the scrape.

4. Kill the germs. Once you've removed the surface dirt from the scrape, you need to kill the germs that can cause an infection. The best thing to use is hydrogen peroxide, which you can buy at any drugstore or supermarket. Hydrogen peroxide may sting a little, but it will make sure that the wound is clean. Pour the liquid directly onto the wound. It's going to fizzle and make white, foamy bubbles. This is good. It means the solution is killing any germs that might be in the scrape.

5. Cover the scrape. Now that it's clean, pat it dry with a clean cloth. Don't rinse it with water, and don't use your mother's good towels. Apply an antiseptic ointment. Then cover the scrape with a band-aid or bandage (depending on how big it is). Make sure that the bandage is not so tight that it blocks your circulation.

6. Clean the scrape with peroxide-soaked gauze and change the bandage daily.

7. If the scrape does not feel better in two days, tell an adult and go to the doctor.

Another way to avoid scrapes is by wearing pants and long-sleeved shirts. Most skating is done in the warmer months, though, so it's usually not practical to wear so much clothing. However, skaters often do wear long, baggy shorts and shirts that can cover the knees and elbows.

It's a good idea, whether you're a beginner or a pro, to wear knee and elbow pads. Any pro will tell you that pads must always be worn when you skate on a ramp. The pads are the only thing separating you from the ramp's hard, splintery wood. On the street, pads prevent your elbows and knees from scraping the ground. More important, if you fall very hard, the pads can prevent you from breaking or fracturing your arm or leg.

Elbow and knee pads are usually made of Lycra and cotton. Lycra is the stretchy material often used in exercise clothes. It's tough and durable, but it stretches and bends easily. Inside the Lycra is a hard plastic shell that covers your elbows and knees. These joints must be protected.

Bailmaster John Cardiel loses control of a railslide, with a painful result.

Keep Your Head

Other than your brain, the helmet is the most important piece of safety equipment. A helmet can prevent injury to your skull and brain. Your brain is soft and delicate, and your skull is the one layer of defense between it and the hard ground. Unfortunately, your skull can defend your brain only so much. Skulls can break or fracture just as other bones can. Your brain needs the added protection of a helmet to keep you thinking and skating straight.

If you're not wearing a helmet and you do fall and hit your head, you could fracture your skull, which can cause brain damage. With a helmet your skull is protected. If you do fall and hit your head, you should see a doctor immediately, even if you were wearing a helmet when you fell. If you feel dizzy, have a headache, or experience blurry vision, you might have a concussion. Concussions are temporary disturbances of the brain's functions. They usually don't last long or cause permanent damage, but they need medical attention right away. In rare cases, hitting your head in a fall can cause bleeding inside the brain, which is extremely serious.

Skating is fun, and pulling off the cool tricks feels good, but hurting yourself doesn't. The way not to get hurt is to stay safe and be smart. Wear the right safety gear to protect yourself from the scrapes, bruises, fractures, and breaks. Be smart and don't try to do tricks that are too dangerous or that you're not ready for. Most of all, have fun!

One thing that makes skateboarding a great sport is that you don't need a lot of equipment to get started. You have plenty of choices with both style and comfort, and the main thing to remember when starting out: You won't know until you try. It'll take some use and abuse of your equipment before you know for sure what brands and styles of gear you prefer. Let's break down the three main components:

The Board

The board, or deck, is made from seven thin layers of wood compressed together and sealed with veneer. It's about one-half inch thick and very strong. Some boards have a layer of plastic bonded to the bottom. These are known as slick boards. Boards come in different styles, which have changed over the years to follow various trends. Longboarding, using big, long skateboards, is popular with a small number of skaters nowadays. But in general, today's boards tend to be shorter and narrower than the boards that were popular during the 1970s and '80s.

The back of the board is always curved upward, forming a tail. This tail plays the key part in many tricks. The nose—the front of the board—can also be curved up. Sometimes it is less curved than the tail, and some- times each end is equally curved. The amount of curving in the tail or nose is called the concave. The concave of the board you choose is all about personal preference. Try starting off with a board that is somewhere in the middle. Then, once you start learning tricks, you can decide if you want more or less concave in the tail or nose.

Once you choose a board, you will need to put grip tape over the top of it. This is so your feet don't slip off while you're riding and doing tricks. Usually the store where you buy your board can put it on for you.

Some boards have graphics on the bottom, and some do not. The ones without graphics are usually cheaper. If a board has graphics, it's usually a pro model. If a skater becomes a pro, he or she will be sponsored by one of the major skateboard manufacturers. The manufacturer will pay to put the skater's name on the bottom of the board, just as Michael Jordan was paid to have his name on a pair of Nike sneakers. A graphic makes no difference in the quality of the board, although a lot of pros are also awesome artists and do their own graphics. You may want to skate your favorite pro's board because you admire his or her technique on a vert ramp or with a paintbrush!

Skater Bio

One way for a professional skater to make sure that he's happy with his equipment is to help design it. Chad Muska, one of the most exciting skaters around today, helps design boards at Shorty's Skateboards. Chad, who was born in 1977 and lives in San Diego, may get some of his talent from his father, who designs wheelchairs.

Trucks

The trucks are axles that get bolted underneath the board. The wheels are attached to the trucks. When deciding which trucks to buy, weight is the main consideration. The lighter the trucks, the easier it will be to get airborne when you do tricks. Aluminum trucks are lightweight, but they also can be expensive. Some trucks have plastic base plates. Plastic is light, but it can crack if you are doing hard-core skating with lots of tricks and turns. Choose your trucks based on your budget and how hard you are going to skate. For beginners it's usually best to go for less expensive equipment. That way if you don't like a particular feature of the equipment you've been using, you'll be able to afford new gear.

Wheels and Bearings

Wheels are made from polyurethane, a hard synthetic material. They come in different diameters. The diameter is the measure of how big the wheels are. When skating was gaining popularity in the eighties, big wheels were more popular. Now, smaller wheels sometimes mean bigger tricks. Many professionals skate smaller wheels both in the park and on the street. Today's smaller wheels speed up faster than the old style. They are also somewhat thinner, however, and this makes them less durable for street skating.

Bearings make the wheels move. They are found between the wheel and the axle. Bearings are assigned ABEC ratings. The higher the ABEC rating, the faster the wheels will be. A lower ABEC rating is generally more practical for a beginner. As you get better and more confident, you may want faster bearings for your wheels.

You will choose hardware—bolts for mounting trucks and other parts to the board—when you buy your skateboard. Ask the people working at your local skate shop to recommend the best bolts for your board. It doesn't hurt to have a skate tool either. That's a special kind of wrench you can use to adjust your mounting bolts and wheels. You can pick one up at any skate shop.

By the time you're ready to buy your board, some new styles of boards and wheels will probably be available and popular. Equipment is always changing and evolving. The basics will probably stay the same, but who knows? Maybe in the future there won't be wheels, but antigravity beams suspending you a foot above the ground!

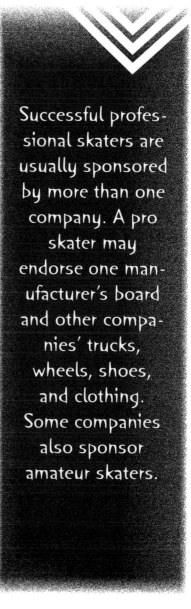

Successful professional skaters are usually sponsored by more than one company. A pro skater may endorse one manufacturer's board and other companies' trucks, wheels, shoes, and clothing. Some companies also sponsor amateur skaters.

What to Wear

Skateboarding has long had an impact on style and fashion. Since there are no uniforms as there are in many other sports, skateboarders have created their own sense of style. You can see examples of skate style being worn in the skate parks as well as on the streets by amateurs, wannabes, and fans of skateboarding alike. Most companies that manufacture skateboards also have an accompanying clothing line consisting of T-shirts, hats, shorts, and pants. Companies such as Airwalk and Vans make sneakers especially for skateboarding. Nonskaters are now wearing these sneakers too.

When you skate it doesn't really matter what you wear. Whole lines of clothing are dedicated to skateboarding, but the differences between brands are more about style than function. Loose-fitting clothing—baggy pants and oversized T-shirts—is the preferred uniform of most skaters today, maybe because baggier clothes are easier to move around in. Styles change all the time, though, and no one knows what the next fashion in skate clothes will be. As for shoes, all you really need are sneakers that aren't too bulky. Avoid clunky basketball sneakers. The most efficient shoes for skaters are tough and lightweight, with flat soles that enable you to feel your board beneath you.

Buying Your Board

Before you go out and buy the latest, most high-tech skateboard on the market, you'll want to try out some different types and brands of boards. If you have friends who skate, ask to try out their boards. That will give you a sense of what you like and don't like. Some bike and board shops will also let you rent boards. If you can, try renting a few different models before you buy. You also can ask the people who work at your local skate shop for recommendations. They will be able to guide you to the right board if you let them know where you plan to skate, how often, and how hard.

Skateboards can be expensive, so if you're not sure you're going to stick with the sport, you may want to consider buying a used board. If you end up getting into skating—and you will—you can trade up to a new board later on. Used sporting goods stores are a great place to find used boards, and you also can ask other skaters if they have old boards that they'd like to sell.

Let's Go!

So you've put together a good board, and you have the right safety gear . . . you're ready to go out and thrash! What's next? It's tempting just to grab a board and jump on a ramp, but it's definitely not anywhere near as easy as the pros make it look! There's more than just balance involved in being able to pull off the big tricks. Skateboarders who are riding professionally today have been riding for years and know what they're capable of. A good number of them have had many broken bones, fractures, and scars to show for their efforts. Although they may not look or feel cool, helmets and pads can save you from abrasions, fractures, broken bones, or even death.

Skaters prepare to drop into the halfpipe.

First, find a place to skate. Your neighbor's drive-way probably isn't the best spot, unless you ask first and the driveway isn't too steep. Neither is any other private property unless you have the owner's permission. Public places where you can get away from large groups of people are your best bet. That way you won't hurt anyone else. You should avoid places like the middle of a busy street, for example, where you are likely to get hurt. Parks are often a good place to start, but make sure that skateboarding is allowed before you try out a new park. If there is a skate park or designated skate area near where you live, check it out. Also try asking around. There are probably other skaters in your neighborhood or at your school. If you ask them, they'll show you the most skater-friendly places. They may even be willing to show you how to pull off the latest tricks, or how to master the basics if you're not ready for anything more. Watch, learn, and most important, practice.

Watching other skaters is one of the best ways to develop your skating

Pro skater Ben Liversedge is grinding his back trucks.

Park It!

Hundreds of skate parks opened in the 1970s—and most of them closed during that decade too. Skate park owners had a hard time affording the parks' insurance policies, and as parks closed, skaters had to practice in the streets and other public areas. During the 1980s, skateboarding was hugely popular, but not much of it took place in skate parks. Then in the 1990s skate parks began to make a comeback. Skateboard manufacturers, skaters, and city governments worked together to make parks acceptable to both skaters and to the public. More and more skate parks are opening across the country, even in places where skating on the street is illegal.

If there's no skate park near where you live, you and your friends who skate might think about making one yourselves. Most skateboarding magazines and many skating Web sites offer plans for building ramps in various sizes and configurations. But starting a skate park isn't as easy as just building a couple of halfpipes, so do your research and make sure you know what you're getting into before you even think about creating your own park. Several companies and organizations work with local governments, community leaders, and skaters to develop and build skate parks. Check the resources listed at the end of this book for more information.

skills. You may have heard that skaters are trouble and that you shouldn't be hanging out with them. The truth is that good skaters are usually too busy skating and learning new tricks to be into anything harmful like drugs, alcohol, or vandalism. If you do know skaters who are into bad behavior, you shouldn't try to learn from them or be friends with them. Use your judgment and try to associate yourself with other skaters who aren't into trouble. Skaters sometimes get a bad rap, but the real ones are athletes who are into taking care of themselves and becoming better skaters. Most of them won't mind taking you under their

wing and teaching you what they've learned. Chances are, someone taught them when they were first trying to learn too. There are a few more things you can do to get started on your way to becoming a skateboarder. Developing your sense of balance is one of the most important. The best way to get used to balancing is to ride around in a part of your neighborhood where there are no cars and few people. That way there's less chance of you or anyone else getting hurt. If you fall off your board, you may hurt yourself, but if you fall off the board and it shoots out from under you at someone else's shins, that isn't too good either. Use your head. Know your limits and take it slow. You're not going to be pulling off big—or even small—tricks right away. Like anything else, skateboarding takes practice.

How High Can You Ollie?

There are so many tricks in skate-boarding, from the easiest to the most complex, that it can be hard to know where to start. If you've never stepped onto a skateboard, you probably think it looks kind of easy. After all, how hard can it be? All those skaters on ESPN make it look simple.

Well, it's not. Those people on television make it look easy because they've been skate-boarding for a long time and prac-ticing every trick until they have it down perfectly. Mark McGwire makes hitting home runs look easy too, but he broke the record only by practicing. And it's the same with skateboarding. With practice you can pull off any trick, but you need a starting point. The first and most important thing to practice is just getting on the board and riding around. This may sound silly, but if

Getting air in Venice Beach,

you've never ridden one before, you may feel a little clumsy.

Starting Out

Once you get used to it, you'll be able to roll all over the place. Find an open area like a schoolyard or a closed parking lot. You want to be where there aren't any cars or people. Practice just rolling from place to place and try to feel the board underneath you. You need to have control of the board—it can't control you. Next try kicking. To kick is to move the board forward by placing one foot on it, toward the front, and pushing on the ground with your other foot. If you are right-handed, you'll probably want to kick with your left foot. Try kicking a few times and then putting your foot back on the board and rolling around. If you are left-handed, you'll want to kick with your right foot. In skateboarding this is called "goofy-foot." It's not really goofy or otherwise unacceptable; it's just that there are more right-handed people out there, so there are more skaters who use their left foot to kick. Use whichever foot you feel most comfortable with. You'll know right away which one you want to use.

Practice kicking and rolling until you've got it down. Be careful of even the smallest pebble on the ground. Until you get used to the way the

skateboard feels, even a tiny little rock getting stuck under the wheel can make it stop. This will make you fly forward and land on your face. Ouch.

Once you've mastered kicking and rolling, try kicking harder to make yourself go faster. Not too fast, though—for most tricks you don't need to go too fast. Skateboarding is more about control than speed.

Beyond the Basics: Ollies and More

Once you feel as though you've got these basics down, you're ready to try a few tricks. The first trick is all about balance. Balance is the key element to mastering any skateboarding trick. In an open space, get a little speed and try balancing on the back two wheels—just like a wheelie on a bicycle. Try doing it for a few seconds at a time. It's hard at first, but keep trying until you can do it for a couple of seconds and keep on rolling without falling off. This exercise will help you gain balance and an understanding of the way a skateboard moves.

All tricks in skateboarding are based on the ollie. The ollie is the first trick to learn once you've learned to control the board. The ollie lets you raise the board up off the ground through a sequence of foot and body motions. It's a trick that requires balance, agility, and coordination. It sounds hard, but once you practice and get it down, it will be second nature. In the ollie, you force the board to pop up under your feet and jump while you jump. It looks as if the board is attached to your feet, which of course it isn't.

If you don't have anyone to show you how to ollie, start by following these steps. Reverse the foot directions if you skate goofy-foot.

1. Practice jumping gently and landing back on the board. Be careful to make sure that the board doesn't fly out from underneath you. After you feel confident with your foot position, you're ready to try the ollie.

2. With the board stopped, place your right foot on the tail of the board and your left foot a little below the center.

3. Now here's the hard part. These next things have to happen simultaneously. Stamp down with your right foot while sliding your left foot up the board toward the nose and jumping into the air.

It sounds hard, but with practice you'll get it. Keep at it. Master this trick, and you are ready for anything. Once you learn to ollie while standing still, you can try doing it while moving.

When you're learning to ollie, you're going to fall down a lot. If you don't fall down at first, you're not trying hard enough. You need to fall down in order to gain an understanding of the way the skateboard works. Once you learn to ollie while moving, you can ollie onto curbs and over almost anything. Soon you can use your ollies on ramps at skate parks and over obstacles on courses or on the street. Learning the ollie is the beginning of

Beyond the Ollie

If you watch experienced skaters, you'll quickly discover that there are almost as many names for tricks as there are skaters, and that any two skaters might each do the same trick in a slightly different way. These are some of the most common tricks you're likely to see:

The Nollie: Like an ollie, but the skater uses the nose instead of the tail to make the board pop up.

The No Comply: Another variation on the ollie in which the skater's front foot slides off the heel edge of the skateboard as the front of the board flips up. In a no comply, the skater can go over taller obstacles than in an ollie.

The Kickturn: In a kickturn the skater raises the front wheels up off the ground or ramp surface, pivots 180 degrees on the back wheels, and sets the front wheels down.

The McTwist: A rotation of 540 degrees in midair, done backside. Other rotations are referred to by degree. You'll see people doing frontside or backside 180s and 360s, and some expert skaters can even pull off a 720.

advanced skateboarding. After learning this trick, you're ready to try ollie kickflips, which is an ollie as usual, but the board flips around under your feet before you land back on it. Once you've mastered the ollie and ollie kickflips, you'll probably start inventing your own variations on these tricks.

Other parts of the skateboard also can be used for tricks. A "grind" involves sliding on a curb or railing on the trucks instead of the wheels. A grind can be either a trick by itself or combined with a series of tricks. For example, you could do an "ollie kickflip to grind."

When you've learned all the ollie-based tricks, you can try everything "backside." Most tricks you'll try are done while facing in the same direction as you're moving. When you're facing the other way and do the same trick backward, it's called backside instead of frontside. The possibilities for tricks seem endless, and new ones are being created all the time.

Watch your fellow skaters and the pros at competitions to keep up with all the new tricks. You'll be doing them in no time!

Taking out the trash: Ben Liversedge does a huge ollie-flip.

7

Park vs. Street: Two Worlds

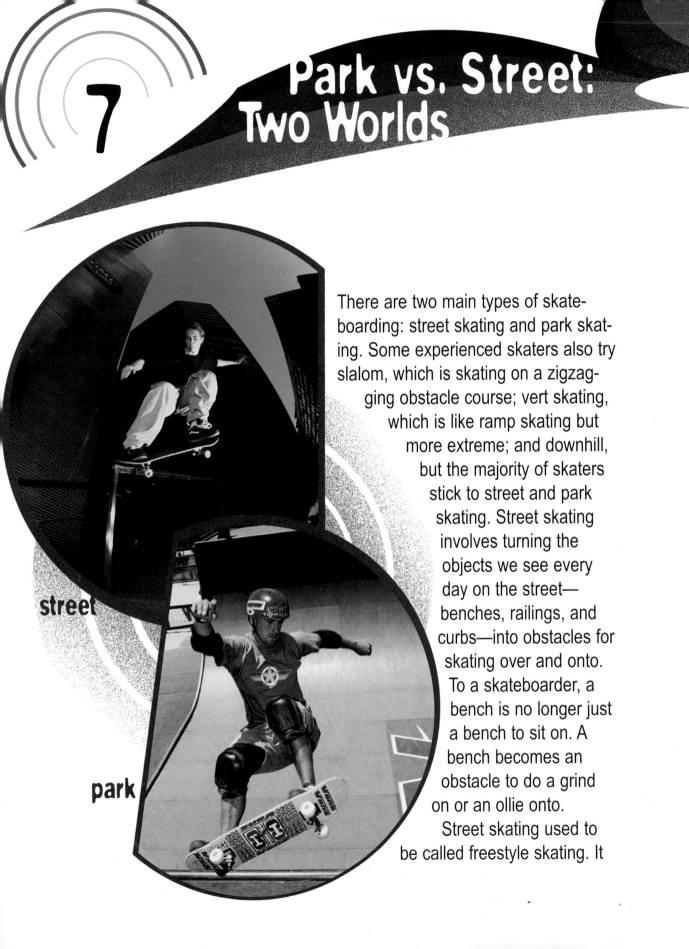

street

park

There are two main types of skate-boarding: street skating and park skating. Some experienced skaters also try slalom, which is skating on a zigzagging obstacle course; vert skating, which is like ramp skating but more extreme; and downhill, but the majority of skaters stick to street and park skating. Street skating involves turning the objects we see every day on the street—benches, railings, and curbs—into obstacles for skating over and onto. To a skateboarder, a bench is no longer just a bench to sit on. A bench becomes an obstacle to do a grind on or an ollie onto.

Street skating used to be called freestyle skating. It

was done with smaller, narrower boards called freestyle boards. Nowadays these boards are not very popular (though some freestylers are still around), and most street skaters use wider boards. Street skating involves a lot of ollies, combinations of ollies, and other tricks such as kick-flips and backsides.

Park skating involves ramps such as halfpipes and quarter-pipes. A halfpipe, which is a chute with high, U-shaped walls, is the most popular type of skateboarding ramp. Vert ramps are halfpipes with an extra section of vertical wall—that means skaters are riding straight up and down!

Halfpipes are so popular that freestyle bike riders and in-line skaters are now using them. Skaters go up and down the halfpipe pulling off tricks. Tricks are performed on the lip, or edge, of the ramp

and in the air above the lip. (The lip is also called the coping.)This is probably the most exciting style of skating to watch. You never know what's going to happen next.

Downhill skateboarding has continued to grow in popularity. As you can guess from the name, it involves riding a board downhill—as fast as possible. Downhill skating is exciting to watch and to do, but it's also risky. Only experienced skaters should try it.

Many skaters also snowboard—which is similar to surfing on snow just as skateboarding is a kind of sidewalk surfing—during the winter, and amateurs and pros compete in both sports.

In the past, skaters usually specialized in either park or ramp style, but most skaters nowadays like both. For you it may depend on what is available in the area where you live. Many towns have skate parks, but they may be expensive or reserved for the advanced amateurs and professionals in the neighborhood. Often, however, skate parks offer lessons on half-pipe skating. Go for it! It's fun and rewarding.

So you've found the board you like the best. You've practiced every day, and you've become pretty good. You can skate better than anyone in your neighborhood. What's next? The next step is to show off what you've learned in competitions. Competitions are what turn amateurs into professionals. Competitions separate the weekend skater from the hard-core extreme athlete.

Competitions come in many forms, from your local community-sponsored competitions to international corporate-sponsored events. Big money and fame await those who make it to the top. But as is true of any sport,

The street course at the 1998 X Games in San Diego, California

Skater Bio

Elissa Steamer is a young skater from Huntington Beach, California. Elissa, who skates with the Toy Machine team, started skating when she was twelve years old. She became a professional skateboarder in 1998.

only the very best get there. Only through practice, passion, and determination do the best pros make it to this level.

Whether you have dreams of becoming a professional skateboarder or if you just want to see how extreme you can be, competitions are the way to go. To begin competing as an amateur, you'll need to check with your local skateboarding community. There are skate shops in almost every town across the country. Many shops sponsor their own local competitions. Enter these and if you win, you could be eligible to qualify for regional competitions. Regional competitions are usually broken down by city or town. If you win one of these, you can go to a national competition and beyond. Unlike most

The first major skateboarding competition was the First International Championships, held in Anaheim, California, in 1965. The event was shown on network television throughout the United States.

other sports, skateboarding doesn't have a single governing agency that organizes competitions worldwide. There are so many different competitions each year that it's hard to keep track of them all. The International Association of Skateboard Companies (IASC) and World Cup Skateboarding organize some of the best-known competitions.

Numerous competitions are happening all over the world. Look at

Tail grind on the coping: A skater attacks the mighty vert ramp at the 1997 X Games.

Skaters from all over the world wow a huge crowd at the 1998 X Games.

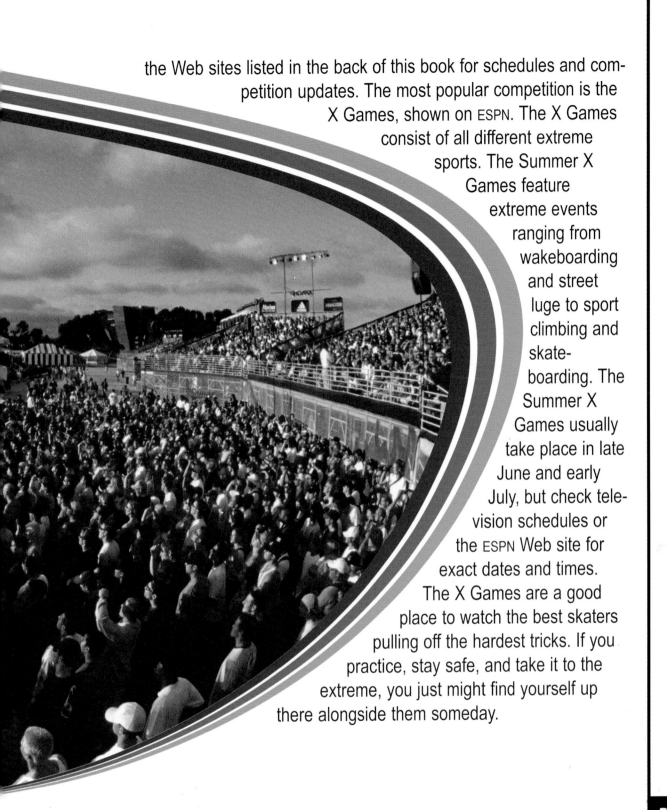

the Web sites listed in the back of this book for schedules and competition updates. The most popular competition is the X Games, shown on ESPN. The X Games consist of all different extreme sports. The Summer X Games feature extreme events ranging from wakeboarding and street luge to sport climbing and skateboarding. The Summer X Games usually take place in late June and early July, but check television schedules or the ESPN Web site for exact dates and times. The X Games are a good place to watch the best skaters pulling off the hardest tricks. If you practice, stay safe, and take it to the extreme, you just might find yourself up there alongside them someday.

X-Planations

backside Doing a trick backside means starting with the back end of your board facing forward.

bail Falling or dropping your board mid-trick, on purpose or on accident.

bearings A part inside the wheels of a skateboard that makes the wheels roll smoothly.

concussion A usually temporary injury to the brain resulting from a fall or blow to the head.

fakie Backward. Skating fakie means skating backward.

frontside Doing a trick frontside means starting with the front end of your board facing forward.

goofy-foot Skating with your right foot forward. Most people skate "regular," with their left foot forward.

grab Grabbing the board with your hand while doing an ollie.

grind Skating on the edge of an object such as a curb, park bench, or handrailing.

grip tape A rough material with adhesive on one side that is attached to the top of a skateboard for better traction.

halfpipe A type of skateboarding ramp with U-shaped walls.

kickturn A trick that involves spinning on the rear wheels of the skateboard with the front wheels lifted off the ground.

lip The upper edge of a skateboarding ramp; also called coping.

nose The front end of the skateboard.

old school Usually refers to the tricks, styles, boards, and skaters of the 1980s who made the sport popular.

ollie   The basis of most skateboarding tricks. An ollie involves making the skateboard pop up underneath you, with all four wheels off the ground as you jump into the air.

park skating   Skateboarding that takes place in skate parks on halfpipes and other ramps.

rail slide   Sliding on a curb or handrail on the slick underside of the board.

sick   Cool, extreme; used to describe a well-executed trick.

street skating   Skateboarding that takes place on planned courses, in parks, or on the street. Also called freestyle skating.

tail   The back end of the skateboard.

vert   Vertical; skating on a ramp that has a vertical wall.

Extreme Info

Web Sites

Axoskate.Com—Ultimate Skateboarding Site
http://www.axoskate.com

Blender Skateboarding (on line zine)
http://www.members.tripod.com/~blenderskatemag/index.html

CCS Mailorder Skateboards and Snowboards
http://www.ccsmailorder.com
You can order boards, trucks, wheels, tools, and accessories at this mail order
site, or you can just request a catalog of all the products they sell.

DansWORLD: Skateboarding
http://web.cps.msu.edu/~dunhamda/dw/dansworld.htm
This site features lots of useful information, including links to skateboarding FAQS
and a personal history of skateboarding.

ESPNET Sports Zone
http://www.espn.com
Follow the links to the X Games skateboarding pages, and you'll find anything
and everything you need on the X Games skateboarding events.

Extreme: Skateboarding zone
http://www.zinezone.com/zones/extreme/skateboarding/index.html

Filters Magazine
http://www.ideograf.com/filters
An on-line zine for new and experienced skaters.

Giant Robot
http://www.giantrobot.com
An on-line zine featuring photos, interviews, and tips.

Heckler Magazine
http://www.bayinsider.com/partners/heckler/default.htm
You can read current and past issues of *Heckler* or subscribe to Heckler's e-mail zine at this site.

Jordan's Elite Sk8 Page
http://surf.to/sk8x
This is a well-designed and informative personal home page. It contains product reviews, chat topics, a listing of skate parks, and lots of links.

Pacific Skateboarding Online Magazine
http://www.pacificskateboarding.com

Skateboarding.Com
http://www.skateboarding.com
This site contains a huge number of skateboarding resources, listings, news, competition updates, skating how-tos, tips and tricks, and other links to good skateboarding sites. If you're looking for basic and thorough information, this is a great place to start.

Skateboarding—Great Sports
http://www.greatsports.com/skateboarding

Skateboard.Net
http://www.skateboard.net

Skater.Net
http://www.skater.net

Skatespot.com
http://www.skatespot.com

SkateTalk Skate Chat
http://www2.skatetalk.com/skatetalk

Smirk Magazine
http://www.smirkmagazine.com

SurfLink
http://www.surflink.com/skate
This site features lots of information as well as a history of skateboarding, organized by decade.

Transworld Skateboarding Magazine Online
http://www.skateboarding.com/magazine

Where to Play

Skate Parks

There are skate parks in just about every state and province in the United States and Canada. Skateboarding.Com (http://www.skateboarding.com) has a good list of skate parks, and you can find reviews of different parks in most skate zines.

Many manufacturers of skateboards and skating accessories are working with cities and towns across the country to plan and build skate parks. For more information, contact:

International Association of Skateboard Companies (IASC)
P.O. Box 37
Santa Barbara, CA 93116
(805) 683-5676
Fax: (805) 967-7537
e-mail: nosewriter@aol.com
Web site: http://www.skateboard.com/iasc

You can find another good list of skate parks at:

Skate Park Information
www.rcsboardshop.com/skate-info.html

Skateparks International Home Page
http://www.sk8parks.com

Skate Camps

Tahoe Extreme Sports Camp
P.O. Box 3297
Olympic Valley, CA 96146
(800) PRO-CAMP (776-2267)
Web site: http://www.800procamp.com

Visalia YMCA Skate Camp
211 West Tulare Avenue
Visalia, CA 93277
(209) 627-0700
Fax: (209) 739-7816
Web site: http://sequoialakeymca.com

Windell's Skateboard Camp
P.O. Box 628
Welches, OR 97067
(800) 765-7669
e-mail: windcamp@teleport.com
Web site: http://www.windells.com

Woodward Camp
(814) 349-5633
e-mail: office@woodward.com
Web site: http://www.woodwardcamp.com/xcamp.htm

Competitions

There are almost as many amateur skateboarding competitions as there are skateboarders. If you're interested in competing against other skaters, visit the nearest skate park or check your favorite zine to find out the dates and other details of upcoming skating events.

The best-known professional skating competitions include the X Games, Vans World Tour and Vans Triple Crown of Skateboarding, the B3 (Bikes, Boards, and Blades) Competition, and events organized by World Cup Skateboarding (wcs). For information on wcs events, contact:

World Cup Skateboarding
P.O. Box 836
Soda Springs, CA 95728
(530) 426-1552
Fax: (530) 426-1500
Web site: http://www.wcsk8.com

Extreme Reading

Andrejtschitsch, Jan, Raimund Kallee, and Petra Schmidt. *Action Skateboarding.* New York: Sterling Publishing Co., 1992.

Christopher, Matt. *Skateboard Tough.* Boston, MA: Little, Brown and Co., 1994.

Gutman, Bill. *Skateboarding.* New York: St. Martin's Press, 1997.

Hill, Laban. *Half Pipe Rip-Off.* New York: Hyperion, 1998.

Jay, Jackson. *Skateboarding Basics.* Danbury, CT: Children's Press, 1996.

Leder, Jane. *Learning How: Skateboarding.* Marco, FL: Bancroft-Sage Publishing, 1992.

Lund, Bill. *Extreme Skateboarding.* Danbury, CT: Children's Press, 1997.

Ryan, Pat. *Extreme Skateboarding.* Mankato, MN: Capstone Press, 1998.

Shoemaker, Joel. *Skateboarding Streetstyle.* Danbury, CT: Children's Press, 1996.

Magazines

Box
P.O. Box 56327
Boulder, CO 80322-6327
(800) 999-3269
Web site: http://www.petersenco.com/mag

Thrasher
P.O. Box 884570
San Francisco, CA 94188-4570
(415) 822-3083
Web site: http://www.thrashermagazine.com

Transworld Skateboarding
P.O. Box 469006
Escondido, CA 92046-9986
(888) 897-6247
Web site: http://www.skateboarding.com/magazine

Videos

Skateboarding may have produced more videos than any other sport. There are videos showing trick tips, highlighting the pros' best moves, and celebrating skate culture. Many skateboard manufacturers, including Santa Cruz, Birdhouse, Shorty's, and others, produce their own videos. Your local skate shop or your favorite mail-order catalog should stock all the latest and greatest videos. Magazines such as *Thrasher* and *Transworld* also offer their own videos, including some instructional tapes for beginners.

A company called 411 produces a video "magazine" for skaters. Look for 411 videos at skate shops or contact:

411
1351A Logan Avenue
Costa Mesa, CA 92626
(714) 641-7037

Index